I0473639

# The Complete Guide to Getting a Tattoo for the First Timer

## Sean Hobden

ISBN: 1478393068
ISBN-13: 978-1478393061

# DEDICATION

This book is dedicated to Lloyd Josh and Sofia

Also available on Amazon by Sean Hobden

The Secret of Winning a Tattoo Apprenticeship

The Complete Guide to Getting a Tattoo for the First Timer

# CONTENTS

ACKNOWLEDGMENTS

The tattoo on the front cover was tattooed by Josh Hobden

Facebook: Josh Hobden tattooist

You Tube : Body Art Tunbridge Wells

The Complete Guide to Getting a Tattoo

For The First Timer

Introduction

Today there are so many tattooists and tattoo shops, tattoo designs, tattoos are everywhere, the choice is overwhelming and confusing for the first timer. This guide attempts to answer any questions somebody thinking of getting a tattoo may have, from the obvious question of does it hurt? (yes it does) to choosing the right design, the right placement, and the right tattooist for them in an honest and concise way.

Warning! Getting tattooed can be very addictive. Good luck on your journey.

## Chapter One

## Choosing a Tattoo Design

Basically there are three types of tattoo design, firstly your own design that you take to the tattooist, secondly the tattooists designs that they display on their walls or in their books, in the trade these standard "off the peg" designs are called "Flash", and lastly custom designs that are drawn just for you by the tattooist.

Your own design can be anything taken from anywhere, it could be a logo on a football programme or a design taken from a T shirt, CD or DVD cover, it could be from a magazine, book or even a greetings card, the options are unlimited. Take your time, keep your eyes and mind open and maybe the design will find you.

When you take your design to your tattooist it's best to take it printed on paper, in an ideal world the actual size you want it tattooed but if this is not possible your tattooist will usually advise what size is best and then reduce or enlarge it on their photocopier. Often the tattooist will make a drawing or trace parts from this design you have brought in so it's not a good idea to show your tattooist designs on your mobile phone, as he/she won't be able to do this. From now on I will refer to tattooist's as "he" although I do mean he or she.

If it's a portrait your having done head and shoulders usually works best, take in professionally taken photographs, if it's children school photos work well. Take in as many photos as you can, the tattooist will have more choice as to which photo will translate best into a tattoo. Remember the better the reference the tattooist has the better the tattoo result will be.

A common mistake is to take in designs that are too small especially lettering. Take into consideration that all tattoo lines spread under the skin over time so any lines that are nearly touching will be touching in the future. The written word can be physically tattooed very tiny but when every line touches its neighbour in the future you will end up with a solid grey box. It was a common mistake of tattooists in the 1980's to do tattoo designs too small. Tattoo designs that last the test of time the best and are still "readable" fifty years later are the traditional designs, if you look at a traditional design there are no two lines anywhere near each other so when all the lines spread over time no two lines touch and you still have a readable tattoo. So be realistic with sizing, generally the bigger the design the better the tattoo will be, I appreciate not everybody wants large work especially some women but in my opinion any tattoo that is smaller than fist size will not look good in years to come. Having said that it's your tattoo and you need to feel comfortable wearing it so the golden rule is if it feels too big it is too big and if it feels too small it is too small.

A popular choice is to have lettering tattooed in a foreign language especially Chinese or Japanese but if they are tattooed in a place that is on show be prepared for people to continually ask, "what does that mean?" or "what does that say?" this can get very tiring when it's happening all summer and is going to happen for the rest of your life!

Beware of "gimmicky" or novelty designs, although it's pretty obvious tattoos are for life some people just can't get their heads around it and make a bad choice. It might make your friends laugh now but when the novelty wears off you have to live with it for the rest of your life.

As for getting your partners name I don't want to spoil a romantic gesture or sound like I am preaching so all I will say is that there is a very wise saying in the trade; "tattoos last longer than romance". Of course tattoos are very personal and at the end of the day it's the individuals choice.

Tattoo flash is a good choice of design because these designs are specifically drawn to be tattooed taking into consideration the "rules" of not putting too much detail in too smaller space while as printed designs and logos do not have to take these "rules" into consideration. What puts a lot of people off of flash is that they feel they will have the same design as many other people but if you like flash consider this, nearly everybody wears jeans even people that claim to be very individual, why do they all wear jeans? Because they are good!

Some people won't pick a design off of the wall because a few people may already have it but ironically they will take in a design from the internet that millions and millions have!

Don't forget if you really do like flash you can always ask your tattooist to change the colours, lose parts of it, change parts of it, add other parts from different designs this will make the design "custom".

We now come to the custom design. The custom design is where you and your tattooist work together on a unique design just for you. First you will need a consultation to discuss size, artwork, placement, how it will work and flow and of course the price. Don't go to your tattooist saying, "I like your work but I don't know what I want", if you don't know what you want how is he going to know what you want? They need at least a starting point or an idea but preferably as much reference as possible, the more reference and ideas you take in the more the tattooist will be "fired up" and be inspired to work with you. You always need to "Gel" with your tattooist but even more so with custom tattooing as you are working together on a project. Most tattoo shops don't charge for a consultation, after the consultation and after the price and everything has been agreed the tattooist then takes a deposit for a firm appointment; the deposit comes off of the agreed price of the tattoo. If you need to see and approve the drawings before your appointment some tattooists charge a fee for this but a lot of custom tattooists prepare the drawings the night or morning before your appointment and may also pen a lot straight onto the skin making any required alterations on the day of your appointment.

The next thing to think about after you are sure of your design is placement. If it is your first tattoo the first thing you may want to think about placement is the pain. Do tattoos hurt? Yes they do but it is bearable otherwise nobody would have them done and certainly nobody would go back a second time. What does it feel like? It is a unique sensation that you cannot describe. You will only know by being tattooed. Most "bar room experts" will either say "it doesn't hurt at all" or "it's agony" of course the truth is somewhere in the middle, be prepared for the worst and hopefully it won't be as bad as you think.

Some places hurt more than others. The arms are the easiest place with the underarms more sensitive. The ribs are one of the worst places, back, chest, stomach and feet are also quite painful. Every body's pain threshold is different and some people find different places hurt more or less than other people. Tattoos only hurt while they are being done as soon as the tattooist stops to re ink the pain stops. There is no after pain with the exception of soreness that feels a bit like sunburn.

If you are a young woman take into consideration that tattoos on your stomach will stretch with your stomach when you become pregnant and then when your stomach returns to how it was before the pregnancy in some cases your tattoo could look quite distorted.

There are some places on the body where tattoos just do not work. One such place is down the side of the hand, the problem with the side of the hand is that the ink does not take very well and more often than not just drops out, if it all fell out it wouldn't be so bad but usually half of it drops out and the other half stays in so that it can look terrible, of course there is always the exception to the rule and you may be lucky and it all stays in perfect. Despite this the side of the hand is often requested to be tattooed, most good tattoo shops refuse to do it point blank, some reluctantly do it but make it clear they will not guarantee the work and others either don't care they just want your money and are not thinking of their shops future reputation for quality work and others are simply inexperienced and don't even know it's not a good place to tattoo. The side of the foot is the same where you have dead skin also the bottom of the toes, the top of the foot is fine although a bit painful. Traditional lettering across the fingers works although a wedding band around the finger tends to "spread" and is not a good idea. Serious tattoo shops that do quality work hate this kind of "gimmicky" work and usually refuse to do it by having a very high minimum charge equal to their hourly rate, ironically the tattooists who are the most skilled to do this kind of work refuse while the less skilled will gladly do it, again there is always the exception to the rule.

Be very careful about getting your hands and neck tattooed as it may not be good for your future job prospects, in fact some people who claim benefits as a lifestyle choice get their face, hands and neck tattooed to deliberately make themselves unemployable. Your hands and neck should be your last tattoos not your first ones.

Chapter Two

Choosing a Tattooist

Never be tempted to be tattooed by an unqualified, unlicensed tattooist working from home, the price may be low but you are seriously risking your health. In the trade these types of "tattooist" are called "scratchers". Although their prices are low in the short run, they are actually more expensive in the long run.

Consider the following two scenarios. The first scenario a man goes to a recommended quality tattoo shop, he has studied his chosen tattooists portfolio carefully, he presents his tattooist with bare skin, he pays the going rate for his tattoo, no more, no less. He has a tattoo that he is really proud of and wants to wear a vest to show it off.

Now consider the second scenario. A man has been told that he knows a friend of a friend that does "cheap" tattoos from his house, the "tattooist" working from home says he used to work in a shop and he is good (these people will say anything to get their hands on your precious skin). The scratcher does a terrible job that has obviously been done by an amateur. The man hates his tattoo, makes sure it is always covered when he goes out and cannot live with it so he goes to the recommended quality shop to get it covered. The professional tattooist has to charge him more than he normally charges because there is a lot more work covering a tattoo than working on bare skin. The final result is better than the scratchers tattoo but not as good as he would have done if the man had gone to him in the first place even though he has paid more. He has now paid in total, the scratchers "low" price plus the professional's price that is above his normal price. He has now paid more than the man in the first scenario and his tattoo is not as good! The types of people that fall victim to scratchers are usually unrealistic twice. Firstly they expect the scratcher to do a job as good as a professional and then secondly they expect a professional to wave a magic wand and make their bad tattoo go away. Never ever trust your skin to a scratcher and remember the saying in the trade "cheap tattoos are not good, good tattoos are not cheap".

Now you have decided not to go to a scratcher the serious business begins of choosing your tattooist. Always choose your tattooist by the quality of their work not by the price, remember one quality tattoo that everybody admires is better than having many tattoos that look like they have been done in jail.

 Your first port of call is the Internet. Take your time, do your research, study every tattooist's portfolio for a style you like and then make a short list of shops to visit. Ask yourself how long the shop has been established, if it's a new shop it doesn't mean it's bad but if it's been there a long time it usually means they must be doing something right or at least they've been there long enough for you to ask around about their reputation. It's not only the quality of the artwork remember you need to "gel" with your tattooist, so you want a tattooist with a good cheerful positive attitude. Phone them and see what their phone manner is like. Do they sound friendly and positive? Do they take the time to talk to you if they are busy? If they have a receptionist have they taken the time to train them properly and be interested in your enquiry? Next take the time to visit the shop. First impressions, is the shop bright and professional from the outside? When you go inside are the staff friendly and make you feel welcome? If you get bad vibes leave and move on to the next one.

When you are out and about if you see some real quality work that you like the look of on somebody don't be afraid to approach them and ask them who did it, you will be surprised how much people wearing quality work like to talk about their tattoos, if the artist is local you will hear their name time and time again put them on your list of shops to visit.

Generally speaking a tattooist doing real quality work has been doing it long enough to work to a very high hygienic standard but if you want your mind put at rest don't be afraid to ask about hygiene procedures, a good tattooist will be happy to go through it with you, a tattooist with attitude won't, again if you get any attitude from the tattooist walk. All tattoo shops in the UK have to display their licence, ask to see it. A tip some restaurant guides give is to visit the toilet, if the toilet is clean and well maintained then usually the kitchen and everything else is ok, this tip could apply to tattoo shops as well.

If you like the shop ask for a consultation, these are generally free in most tattoo shops. Now is a good time to ask about any concerns you may have about hygiene procedures, give all your ideas to the tattooist, is he real keen and enthusiastic to do your design? Or is he totally uninspired and uninterested?

If he is uninterested leave, if he is interested ask the price. Make sure you get a firm price not an estimate. For custom work most tattooists charge by the hour. When creating art it's not customary to try and bargain on the price but you are within your rights to ask exactly how many hours the job will take and get a confirmation that the tattooist will stick to his quoted price even if he has underestimated and goes over the quoted time. If you are having smaller work this is done in one sitting and priced by the job, again it's not customary to bargain on the price but if you have a limited budget and you disclose the maximum you are prepared to spend most tattooists will do their best to try and help you, in some cases you can get more than your moneys worth by "showing your hand first". Once everything has been agreed the tattooist will usually ask for a non refundable deposit, this is usually anything up to around 50% of the price of the tattoo. Ask about their rescheduling policy. Most shops understand that things in life can crop up so you may need to reschedule, some shops require twenty four hours notice and others forty eight hours or more make sure you know or you will lose your deposit and go back to the end of the waiting list! When making your appointment you will get an appointment quicker if you are more flexible, evenings and weekends are always more popular and always fill up first so if you can make it at a more "off peak" time such as a Monday morning you will get a space much quicker.

Chapter Three

The Big Day

So the final day has come the day of your first tattoo. It goes without saying don't be late for your appointment, arrive in plenty of time. Make sure you have a good breakfast or at least something to eat before your appointment, your body needs your blood sugar levels up to cope with the stress and pain. It's also a good idea to take a bottle of water or an energy drink with you. Don't be tempted to have a few alcoholic drinks before your appointment, it will not feel any easier in fact it actually feels a bit worse, your blood becomes very thin when you have been drinking alcohol and flows out a lot more during the tattooing process this causes the tattooist to continually wipe it away causing much more soreness. If you show your tattooist disrespect by turning up drunk he will refuse to tattoo you, and if he starts to tattoo you without realising you have been drinking when it becomes apparent he will show you the same disrespect by doing your tattoo as quick as he can to get you out, even though a good tattooist usually does consistent good work you will not be getting their best work, just remember a bad tattooist can't do a good tattoo but a good tattooist can do a bad tattoo! Also think about what you are going to wear, the tattooist needs easy and free access to the part of your body he is going to work on, you would be surprised to know the amount of people that know they are having a tattoo on their leg but turn up in tight jeans, can't roll their trouser leg up and need to completely take their trousers off when they could have easily have worn baggy shorts instead. Wear older clothes that you don't mind getting a bit of ink on, although most tattooists work very cleanly you may get the rare bit of ink spray. Turn up for your appointment clean, going straight to the tattooists from the building site increases the risk of getting dirt in your new tattoo, the tattooist will completely clean the area he is working on but you may get bits of dry dirt deposits in your tattoo from other parts of your body or clothes. If you are having lettering tattooed be prepared, take it with you with the correct spelling written on paper again you will be surprised how many men need to phone their wife to ask how to spell their own children's name or what their child's date of birth is. You will probably have to sign a book or fill in a disclaimer form before your tattooing commences. Now sit back and enjoy the ride! It's very important that you relax and don't tense up, it's easier said than done I know but you can actually halve the pain by relaxing or you can double it by tensing up the choice is yours. The tattooist will now set everything up in front of you. Nowadays everything is prepacked and sterile. Make sure you watch him take a new needle out of the packet and place it through the tube that is also from a packet, he will now attach the tube to the electric motor, in the trade this is called a machine, please don't offend the tattooist by calling it a gun, guns are for shooting people with. He will probably set up two machines one for outlining and one for colouring. The outline hurts more than the colour, but the good news is the outline is the quickest part and it's the first part so it gets easier not worse, there is light at the end of the tunnel. If a tattoo takes around forty minutes the outline will take about five minutes, so you don't have forty minutes of pain you have around five minutes of pain and then around thirty five minutes of it not being too bad. As the tattoo progresses it gets easier and easier as the skin and your body acclimatizes to the pain with the exception of very long sessions that get very sore towards the end. If the tattooist is using everything disposable his only concern is then cross contamination, this is where he touches something with a contaminated hand for example a bottle of ink and then picks this up again when he is tattooing his next client. So that cross contamination doesn't occur the tattooist will not touch things like the phone for example in the first place or if he must touch them he will either take off his gloves, answer the phone and then put on a new pair of gloves or he will cover it in cling film and change the cling film between clients, hence everything in a tattoo studio covered in cling film. Next he will pour out his inks in disposable inkpots using clean gloves. He will then wash and shave the area to be tattooed and then maybe apply a stencil to follow as a rough guide or he may pen guidelines straight onto the skin. He will then apply some cream over the stencil and then proceed to follow the lines, please don't be alarmed if the tattooist doesn't follow the lines of the stencil exactly as they are only a rough guide. If you feel dizzy or faint at any time ask the tattooist to stop, trust me on this the best thing you can do is put your head as low as you can between your knees from a sitting position, the blood will run to your head and you will feel much better, don't come up too soon or the blood will run down again and you will feel the same, when you do come up come up slowly. If you stay down long enough you will not faint. Don't be tempted to go outside for some fresh air, as appealing as this seems you will probably faint and could hit your head on the way down and then wake up with a crowd around you! A joke old school tattooists used to play if you fainted was to put your watch forward two hours and the shop clock forward as well and then when you came round they would say you had been out for hours even though you had been out for five or six seconds!

When the tattooist has finished tattooing you he will cover the tattoo in more cream and then cover it with a dressing or cling film. He will then give you an aftercare card explaining all the does and don'ts. Congratulations you are now one of the tattooed fraternity and are probably planning your next one already.

Chapter Four


Aftercare


After the tattooist has finished he will give you his aftercare advice. Every tattooist's advice is usually different. Aftercare advice is constantly evolving just the same as tattooing is constantly evolving. Here I will give a little bit of aftercare history from thirty years ago to right up to the present day.


In the 1960's and 1970's when a tattooist had finished your tattoo he (I say "he" now because there were very few women tattooing then) would smear Vaseline on your tattoo with an ungloved, ink covered bloody hand, he would then cover it with kitchen roll secured by normal Sellotape. He would then send you on your way telling you not to pick the scab. Some tattooists would fill little pots themselves with Vaseline or some other cream they got from the chemist or the back of a lorry, stack them high with a sign saying "Special Japanese healing Cream two shillings a pot".

This method was done for years. Vaseline is one of the worst things you can put on a new tattoo. Firstly all Vaseline is, is a clear plain grease that does nothing except block the pores of your skin so that it cannot breath, it has no antiseptic healing properties. Secondly and more serious if it is taken from a jar using your fingers and the jar is used by other people you run the risk of cross contamination that could seriously infect your tattoo, never put Vaseline on your new tattoo.

Somewhere in the 1980's Savlon cream became the preferred choice of most tattooists. Around this time some "bright spark" working at a tattooing convention thought if I cover my finished tattoo with cling film rather than a dressing or paper roll everybody will see the work. This idea caught on and it is now the preferred method of covering a tattoo by most tattooists all over the world. However cling film is controversial with some health authorities they say that bacteria can multiply fast under cling film. As it's used all over the world by nearly every tattooist I can't see a problem.

Somewhere in the 1990's Bepanthem cream became the tattooist's choice. Bepanthem cream is a nappy rash cream but don't let that put you off, Bepanthem is used all over the world by tattooists and is even listed in a lot of tattoo supply catalogues. It really is great stuff, it heals a tattoo much faster than everything else and in some cases your new tattoo does not even form a scab. Being a nappy cream it is especially good if your tattoo is on your butt! (Sorry I couldn't resist that one).

Around the late 1990's company's started to appear selling tattoo healing cream manufactured specifically for tattooing, although all these creams are good I personally think Bepanthem is just as good or better.

Where tattooists differ is how long to keep your new tattoo covered for. Different tattooists will tell you to keep it covered with the initial dressing from anything from one hour to twenty four hours. I would say one or two hours is fine but then you need to let the air get to it. Once you have taken the dressing off never recover it, it needs to breath. The first thing you should do after taking off the dressing is to wash it in clean warm soapy water carefully washing off any dried blood or cream, pat dry with a clean towel, do not rub, and then apply a thin layer of Bepanthem. Here's a tip, Bepanthem cream is quite thick so stand the tube in a cup of warm to hot water for about thirty seconds to thin it down a bit, now you can apply a very thin layer just making it shiny and the tube will go much further. Never share the tube with anybody else unless you are very careful to take the cream from the tube without touching the top to avoid cross contamination, this is very serious many people don't realise if you get your tattoo infected, the infection could race through your body very fast and in extreme cases you could very easily lose a limb, this will not happen if you follow aftercare advice properly.

There is a myth that you cannot get your tattoo wet. You should not go swimming until your tattoo is fully healed, neither should you soak it, this I believe is how the myth started. You can have a shower as soon as the dressing is off, a bath is also fine as long as you don't soak your tattoo under water.

Apply cream around three times a day, first thing in the morning when you get up, mid day and then again just before you go to bed, to help you remember do it every time you clean your teeth.

The sun is one of the biggest enemies of tattoos. Keep your new tattoo out of the sun. The sun will cook it and could infect it. You may get a scab on your tattoo after a day or two this is normal and nothing to worry about, you may get a very thin one or a very crusty one depending on how heavy the style of tattoo. Generally line work or light shading doesn't scab much but heavy block colouring does. Do not pick or scratch your new tattoo just let the scab do it's own thing and come off of it's own accord. Be patient sometimes your tattoo will heal but there will be one stubborn part that takes much longer to heal this is where it's been worked a little harder for example a dagger with a solid red part at the tip. It takes around a week to ten days for the scab to come off, and then you get a secondary dry, dead type skin form, at this stage you can apply any moisturiser you like. Depending on the style of work it can take another month or so before the skin is totally smooth. These times are only a very rough guide everybody is different much can depend on your general health, diet, metabolism etc. etc.

Some people experience itching when the shaven hair starts to grow back, never scratch your tattoo, if you must scratch to relieve itching scratch around the tattoo not the tattoo itself. Use your common sense avoid exposing your new tattoo to dirty environments, if you work in a dirty environment do not cover your new tattoo with a dressing just use fairly loose fitting clothing. If you follow the aftercare properly you will not have a problem but if you get an infection in your tattoo for any reason get medical help immediately do not say "I will go to the doctors after the weekend". A quick course of antibiotics will stop the infection in it's tracks providing you do it immediately, if you leave it, it could be potentially life threatening.

Now that your tattoo has fully healed check that no parts have fallen out with the scab, if this has happened go back to your tattooist, but do not go back too early as the skin needs to be completely healed and smooth for him to work on it again. A good tattooist will be happy to do free retouches as they want their work to look it's best and it doesn't happen often but a bad tattooist will try and blame you and want to charge you again as they will always be getting complaints.

Now that your tattoo is fully healed the only thing that will fade your tattoo other than time is the sun. You will notice outdoor manual workers who have very old tattoos on their arms, will have faded tattoos on the top of their forearms but relatively bright ones on the underside even though they were done at a similar time. This is because the top ones have full exposure to the sun while the underside is protected from the sun. You can protect your tattoos by putting on a very high factor sun cream or better still shade them by the roof of a bar!!

Directory of the Most Established Tattooists and Tattoo Shops in the UK

Below is a list of some of the most established tattooists and tattoo shops in the UK. The list is by no means exhaustive and the artists are listed in no particular order apart from region.

Southern England

www.seansbodyart.co.uk

www.harrypottertattooist.co.uk

www.lesskusetattoos.co.uk

www.markpettigrewtattoo.co.uk

www.dinostattooistltd.co.uk

www.electricrose.co.uk

www.gbtattoos.co.uk

www.customtattoo.org.uk

www.andyjaystudios.co.uk

London

www.georgebonetattoos.co.uk

www.andybarbertattooandpiercing.co.uk

www.newwavetattoo.co.uk

www.barrylouvaine.com

North of London

www.alstattoos.com

www.tattoo.co.uk

www.skinstyles.co.uk

www.4-skin.org.uk

**Midlands and the North**

www.midlandstattoo.co.uk

www.tattoomuseum.co.uk

www.tattoos.co.uk

**Scotland**

www.terrystattoostudio.com

ABOUT THE AUTHOR

Sean Hobden has been tattooing for over thirty years. He owns one of the most established tattoo shops in the South East of England. He is a member of the prestigious Old Timers Tattoo Club (Membership by strict invitation only).

WWW.SEANSBODYART.CO.UK

YOU TUBE: BODY ART TUNBRIDGE WELLS

www.ingramcontent.com/pod-product-compliance
Lightning Source LLC
Chambersburg PA
CBHW071600170526
45166CB00004B/1745